This Book Belongs To

_____

More By ▲ ART THERAPY COLORING.COM

Art Therapy Sketch Books & Coloring Books

Sketch Books & Coloring Books For Kids and Toddlers:

- Sketchbook For Kids Ages 4-8: Unicorn Cover
- Sketchbook For Kids Ages 4-8: Dinosaur Cover
- Sketchbook For Kids Ages 4-8: Bulldozer Truck Cover
- Sketchbook For Kids Ages 4-8: Fire Truck Cover
- Sketchbook For Kids: Robot Ninja Cover
- Sketch Pad For Kids: Funny Shark Cover
- Sketchbook For Toddlers: Cute Animal Cover
- Detailed Coloring Books For Kids
- Coloring Book for Kids: 50 Funny Animals
- Coloring Books for Toddlers: 50 Cute Animals
- Truck Coloring Book: 100 Coloring Pages

Sketch Books & Coloring Books For Teens and Tweens:

- Sketchbook For Kids 8-12: Skeleton Cover
- Sketchbook For Kids 9-12: Zombie Cover
- Sketchbook For Kids 9-12: Dragon Cover
- Sketchbook For Tweens: Inspiration Cover
- Sketchbook For Teenagers: Wolf Cover
- Sketchbook For Teenagers: Dragon Cover
- Sketchbook For Teens: Butterfly Cover
- Sketchbook For Teens: Happy Birthday!
- Tween Coloring Book: Cute Animal Designs
- Tween Coloring Book: Zendoodle Animals
- Coloring Books For Teens: Ocean Designs
- Teen Inspirational Coloring Books

Published by:
Art Therapy Coloring
www.arttherapycoloring.com
Image Under License From Shutterstock

Made in the USA
Monee, IL
14 November 2024

70152409R00063